MOM'S CAMPER COOKING

VOL. I

These quick and easy recipes are not only for campers. Busy families and those just learning to cook will love how they make life easier.

by
Rita Hewson

MOM'S CAMPER COOKING VOL. I

by
Rita Hewson

International Standard Book Number: 0-9659390-1-4
Library of Congress Control Number: 2006904899

Photos by Tenny Griffin, Larned, KS

Published in the U.S.A. by
MOM'S PUBLISHING
RR 1 Box 88
Larned, Kansas 67550

Rita Hewson is a farm wife and mother of four. She has been a 4-H leader and a church school teacher for over fifteen years. She is the author of five Christian card games and a children's book titled <u>A is for Abraham</u>. When she is not working at home, working part-time at school, or working at the county extension office, you will find her relaxing while camping with her family.

AUTHOR'S NOTES

I have been working on this cookbook ever since we started camping when our fourth child was a baby. At this time my father-in-law, who lived next to us, had a stroke. We found our lives stressed to the max with our four young children and their grandfather who was no longer well. We had only been on one five day vacation in our twelve years of marriage. As farmers, we never felt that we could leave the endless farm work that needed to be done. My husband saw the need for us to get away from the work and stress. However, being "poor" farmers he knew he could not take a family of six to motels and restaurants. He bought an old camper and we left the farm for three days! The more we went the more we realized life at home was not going to fall apart while we were gone. After a few years, we were camping several weekends in the spring and fall and spending an entire two weeks in August relaxing in the mountains. With these camper recipes you can fix wonderful meals for your family and still enjoy your vacation. These quick and easy recipes will also help you spend less time working in your kitchen at home. It is my prayer that by having a little extra time you will spend it with Jesus, and that you will discover the *joy* of life that only He can give.

Rita Hewson

This book is dedicated to my family.
They like to camp and they like to eat.
I love you, MOM

TABLE OF CONTENTS

BEVERAGES

APPLE TINGLER

2 c. APPLE JUICE
1 c. WHITE GRAPE JUICE
1 c. ORANGE JUICE
3 T. LEMON JUICE

1. Mix ingredients together and serve over ice.
2. Yield 1 quart.

An ice cold drink is so refreshing on a hot afternoon. This fruit drink is such a nice change from the super sweet and carbonated soft drinks we usually grab. Jam packed with nutrients and no sugar added, it will revive your energy after hiking or playing ball with the kids. I have found the apple and orange juices in small cans or boxes that do not need refrigeration so I can easily make up a batch any time.

May the God of hope fill you with all *joy* and peace as you trust in him, so that you may overflow with hope by the power of the Holy Spirit.

Romans 15:13

HOT BUTTERED RUM
(non-alcoholic)

1/2 c. (1 stick) BUTTER
1/2 c. BROWN SUGAR
1 c. VANILLA ICE CREAM, softened
4 tsp. RUM EXTRACT

1. Melt butter. Stir in brown sugar until heated.

2. Pour hot mixture over ice cream. Beat by hand until smooth. Add rum extract.

3. To serve, put 1/4 c. mixture in a cup and add 3/4 c. boiling water. Sprinkle with nutmeg.

4. Yield 1 3/4 cups mix or 7 cups hot buttered rum.

This is an elegant drink—but so easy. I make it at home to take with us camping. It keeps well in the ice chest or refrigerator. It is fun to surprise and delight my friends and family by serving Hot Buttered Rum while camping.

HOT CHOCOLATE MIX

5 c. POWDERED MILK
1 1/2 c. (6 oz.) NON-DAIRY POWDERED
   COFFEE CREAMER
1/2 c. POWDERED SUGAR, unsifted
1 (3.9 oz.) box CHOCOLATE FUDGE
   INSTANT PUDDING MIX
1/2 lb. box (I 1/2 c.) INSTANT CHOCOLATE
   DRINK MIX

1. Mix ingredients together and store in a tightly covered container.
2. Add 1/3 c. mix to 1 c. hot water.
3. Yield 7 cups mix or 21 cups hot chocolate.

How wonderful it is to sit around a warm campfire with a cup of hot beverage or to wrap up in a blanket in the camper during a rain storm with a hot drink to warm your insides. I can feel the peace and contentment just thinking about it. At such times, the scattered family comes together. The card games, dominoes, stories, and laughter will be memories of *joy* forever.

HOT MOCHA MIX

1/2 c. COCOA
1 1/4 c. SUGAR
1 c. POWDERED SUGAR
1 c. POWDERED MILK
1/4 c. INSTANT COFFEE

1. Stir together cocoa and sugar until completely blended.
2. Stir in other ingredients and store in a tightly covered container.
3. Add 1/3 c. mix to 1 c. hot water.
4. Yield 3 cups mix or 9 cups hot mocha.

The hot chocolate mix and the hot mocha mix need to be blended until smooth. The powdered milk and instant coffee are coarse. They will work down easily into fine powders if pressed with the back of a large spoon.

When anxiety was great within me, your consolation brought *joy* to my soul.

Psalm 94:19

5

RUSSIAN TEA

1 c. POWDERED ORANGE BREAKFAST
   DRINK
1 c. SUGAR
1/4 c. INSTANT TEA
1 (5 oz.) pkg. SUGAR SWEETENED
   LEMONADE MIX
1 tsp. CINNAMON
1/2 tsp. CLOVES

1. Stir all ingredients together and store in
   a tightly covered container.
2. Add 2 T. mix to 3/4 cup hot water.
3. Yield 2 1/2 cups mix or 20 cups Russian tea.

I like to have a wide variety of beverages on a camping
trip. Russian Tea is an especially good orange and spicy
hot drink. Besides the drink mixes I make, I keep a
plastic container filled with individual tea and coffee
packets. If you buy the individual packets, the tea and
coffee will stay fresh almost indefinitely. I have also
found an assortment of coffee creamers in individual
packets.

SUMMER PUNCH

1 (10 oz.) can FROZEN STRAWBERRY DAIQUIRI
    CONCENTRATE (non-alcoholic)
2 c. cold WATER
2 (12 oz.) cans GINGER ALE

1. Stir together frozen concentrate and water until concentrate is thawed. Add ginger ale just before serving.

2. Fill glasses with ice and fill with punch.

3. Yield 6 1/4 cups.

Summer Punch is not an everyday drink. I save it for special occasions and serve it to guests. Hospitality to friends and strangers is a way to show them the love of Jesus. Of course, we do not want to be foolish about strangers, but remember what is written in the book of Hebrews.

Do not forget to entertain strangers, for by so doing some people have entertained angels without knowing it.
Hebrews 13:2

WASSAIL

2 qt. (64 oz.) CRANBERRY-APPLE JUICE
   COCKTAIL
3 (3 inch) sticks CINNAMON
1/4 c. BROWN SUGAR
1 tsp. (about 30) WHOLE CLOVES
1/2 tsp. (about 20) WHOLE ALLSPICE

1. Combine ingredients and simmer, covered, for
   15 minutes.

2. May serve immediately or cool 1 hour, remove
   spices (pour through a strainer), and
   refrigerate.

3. Yield 1/2 gallon.

I keep Wassail in the refrigerator throughout the
holiday season—ready to heat up for drop in guests.
The smell itself says welcome. Just like it brings that
special touch to the holidays, it can bring pleasure to a
camping trip. Either take it with you or make it while
you are there right over the campfire.

I bring you good news of great *joy* that will be for all
the people.

Luke 2:10

8

SNACKS

BEAN DIP

1 1/2 c. THICK & CHUNKY SALSA
1 lb. (1/2 large box) PASTEURIZED
   PROCESS CHEESE, cubed
1 (16 oz.) can REFRIED BEANS

1. Heat salsa and cheese, stirring occasionally, until melted and smooth. Stir in refried beans and heat through.
2. Serve hot with tortilla chips.
3. Yield 5 cups.

If you have access to a microwave, the ingredients may be heated together in a large bowl until the cheese is melted. To make more of a meal than a snack, add one pound of ground beef that has been fried and drained. This dip is so well liked, I often take it to carry in dinners. I also take it to friends who have had a death in the family and have many people to feed.

The fruit of the Spirit is love, *joy*, peace, patience, kindness, goodness, faithfulness, gentleness and self-control.

Galatians 5:22

BEAR PARTY MIX

1 (10 oz.) box BEAR SHAPED CINNAMON
    GRAHAM CRACKERS
1 (14 oz.) pkg. DRIED BANANAS, broken into
    pieces
1 (12 oz.) can HONEY ROASTED PEANUTS
1 (16 oz.) bag CANDY COATED CHOCOLATE
    CANDIES

1. Stir all the ingredients together and
   store in a tightly covered container.
2. Yield 11 cups.

Snacks are a must on camping trips. We find ourselves
expending more energy than we do at home and the
fresh air seems to make us hungry all day. Children will
love this Bear Party Mix. It may look like junk food, but
the bananas and peanuts add many nutrients.

Shout for *joy* to the Lord, all the earth. Worship the
Lord with gladness; come before him with joyful songs.
                                                    Psalm 100:1-2

BEEF JERKY

2 lb. LEAN BEEF
1/2 c. SOY SAUCE
2 T. WORCHESTERSHIRE SAUCE
1 tsp. GARLIC POWDER
1 tsp. ONION POWDER
1 tsp. HICKORY SMOKE SALT
1 tsp. PEPPER

1. Slice meat 1/4-inch or thinner. Cut into 1-inch strips.

2. Combine soy sauce, Worchestershire sauce, and dry seasonings.

3. Layer meat in a container, covering each layer with sauce. Cover tightly. Marinate 12-24 hours. Stir occasionally to mix.

4. Dry in a dehydrator at 140° until dry (about 8 hours). To oven dry, set on lowest setting (150°-200°) Lay strips of meat over top oven rack. Place foil on bottom oven rack. Keep oven door cracked to let moisture escape.

BEER NUTS

1 lb. RAW SPANISH PEANUTS
1 c. SUGAR
1/2 c. WATER

1. Combine ingredients together in a non-stick 12-inch skillet. Cook, stirring often, until the water is completely absorbed.

2. Spread sugared peanuts on an ungreased cookie sheet. Line with foil for easy clean up. Bake at 300° for 40 minutes.

3. Once cooled, store in an air tight container.

4. Yield 5 cups.

These taste just like the Beer Nuts you buy in the store, but so very fresh. My problem is that I can't stop eating them once I start. Because peanuts are full of protein, they are wonderful to take on a hike or out in the boat fishing. Our outings often end up longer than expected and it is nice to have something along to tie us over. The Beef Jerky on the previous page is also a good food to put into your snack pack. I like to buy "eye of the round" roast when it is on sale and have the meat market slice it for me. If you have to slice it at home, it will be easier if it is partially frozen.

CARAMEL CORN

3 qt. POPPED CORN
1/2 c. (1 stick) BUTTER
1 c. BROWN SUGAR
3 T. CORN SYRUP
1/4 tsp. BAKING SODA

1. Put popped corn in a large bowl. Shake old maids to the bottom and remove.

2. Melt butter in a saucepan. Add brown sugar and corn syrup. Bring to a rapid boil. Boil one minute.

3. Remove from heat and add baking soda. Stir well.

4. Immediately pour over the popped corn, stirring to coat evenly. Separate into small pieces before completely cool.

5. Yield 1 gallon.

My father would make a large batch of this Caramel Corn every Christmas. Now the tradition is for my husband to make it every New Year's Eve.

CHOCOLATE PEANUT BUTTER FUDGE

1 (14 oz.) can SWEETENED CONDENSED
    MILK
1 c. (6 oz.) MILK CHOCOLATE CHIPS
1 c. (6 oz.) SEMI-SWEET CHOCOLATE
    CHIPS
1 c. PEANUT BUTTER

1. Heat milk on low or in the microwave.

2. Add chocolate chips. Stir until melted.

3. Add peanut butter. Stir until smooth.

4. Pat into a 7x11-inch pan that has been
    sprayed with vegetable oil. Let cool
    completely to set. Will get stiffer overnight.

5. Yield 35 pieces.

Well, we must have our sweets! Caramel Corn and
Fudge are old standards. This fudge is chock-full of
protein from the peanut butter so enjoy. It is a fun
recipe for children. Just watch that they don't
overheat the milk.

GRANOLA BARS

1/3 c. BUTTER
1/3 c. CORN SYRUP
1/3 c. BROWN SUGAR
1 tsp. VANILLA
2 c. GRANOLA, crushed
1 1/2 c. CRISPY RICE CEREAL
1/3 c. MINI SEMI-SWEET CHOCOLATE
    CHIPS, optional

1. Melt butter. Add corn syrup and brown sugar. Bring to a rapid boil. Boil 1 minute.
2. Remove from heat. Wait until boiling has stopped, then add vanilla.
3. Combine granola and rice cereal in a bowl. Pour syrup over and stir until evenly coated. Let cool before adding chocolate chips, or they will melt.
4. Press mixture firmly in a greased 9x13-inch pan. Cool completely before cutting into bars.
5. Yield 14 bars.

PEANUT CLUSTERS

1 (24 oz.) pkg. ALMOND BARK, VANILLA OR
   CHOCOLATE
2 c. (12 oz.) BAKING CHIPS, CHOCOLATE,
   VANILLA, OR BUTTERSCOTCH
4 2/3 c. (24 oz.) SALTED PEANUTS

1. Melt almond bark and chips together in
   the microwave or place in a low oven. Keep
   away from all water. Stir until smooth.

2. Stir in peanuts.

3. Drop teaspoonfuls onto waxed paper. Let cool
   to harden.

4. Yield 5 dozen.

These Peanut Clusters are so good. They are far
superior to any you can buy. I always get compliments
on them. The chocolate bark/butterscotch chips
combination is my family's favorite, but they are all
delicious. This is a recipe that children can easily make
on their own. It is foolproof. If the mixture is too thin
to drop into nice mounds, let it cool a little to thicken.

PEOPLE CHOW

3/4 c. (1 1/2 sticks) BUTTER
2 c. (12 oz.) SEMI-SWEET CHOCOLATE
    CHIPS
1 c. PEANUT BUTTER
12 c. (12 oz.) RICE/CORN SQUARE CEREAL
1 (2 lb.) sack POWDERED SUGAR

1. Melt butter. Add chocolate chips, stirring to melt. Stir in peanut butter.

2. Pour chocolate mixture over cereal. Stir to coat evenly.

3. Place about 1/5 of the coated cereal in a large bowl and cover with powdered sugar. Stir gently with spoon or fingers until cereal pieces are covered with powdered sugar.

4. Remove dusted pieces to waxed paper. Let cool and dry. Repeat with remaining coated cereal. Store in a tightly covered container.

5. Yield one gallon.

PICKLED SAUSAGES

1 lb. fully cooked LITTLE SMOKED
   SAUSAGES
1/2 c. SUGAR
1 c. APPLE CIDER VINEGAR
1/2 c. WATER
1 tsp. SALT
2 tsp. PICKLING SPICE
2 tsp. CRUSHED RED PEPPER

1. Put sausages into a one quart jar.

2. Combine sugar, vinegar, water, salt,
   pickling spice, and red pepper in a
   saucepan. Bring to a boil. Pour over
   sausages. Sausages should be covered
   with liquid. If not, add vinegar.

3. Cover and store in the refrigerator. Shake
   once a day to mix. Ready to eat in 3 days.

Add 4 tsp. red pepper instead of 2 tsp. to make them
hotter. Crushed red pepper is found in the spice
section. When the sausages are gone, try adding 8 hard
boiled eggs to the pickle juice. Delicious!

19

RANCH PARTY MIX

6 c. (6 oz.) CORN/RICE SQUARE CEREAL
1 (12 oz.) pkg. OYSTER CRACKERS
5 c. (6 oz.) SMALL PRETZELS
3/4 c. VEGETABLE OIL
2 T. dried DILL WEED
1 (1 oz.) pkg. RANCH DRESSING MIX

1. Combine cereal, crackers, and pretzels in a large bowl.

2. Stir together oil, dill, and dressing mix. Pour over dry ingredients. Stir gently to coat evenly.

3. Place mixture in a brown paper bag. Fold to close and shake occasionally for 2 hours. Let set for several hours to let the bag absorb excess oil. Store in an air tight container.

4. Yield 1 gallon.

Come, let us sing for *joy* to the Lord; let us shout aloud to the Rock of our salvation.

Psalm 95:1

SMOKED CHEESE BALL

1 (5 oz.) jar OLD ENGLISH SHARP
   PASTEURIZED PROCESS CHEESE SPREAD
1 (3 oz.) block CREAM CHEESE, softened
1 c. (4 oz.) finely shredded MONTEREY JACK
   CHEESE
1/4 tsp. LIQUID SMOKE
1/2 c. chopped WALNUTS

1. Beat cheese spread and cream cheese together until smooth.

2. Add Monterey Jack cheese and liquid smoke. Beat until well blended.

3. Refrigerate until stiff. Form into a ball. Roll in chopped nuts.

4. Cover with plastic wrap. Refrigerate until serving.

5. Yield one ball.

The cheeses mix together better if they are at room temperature. This cheese ball has a wonderful smoked cheese flavor. Everyone I serve it to loves it.

TOFFEE CORN

2 qt. POPPED CORN
1 c. PECAN PIECES
2/3 c. PEANUTS, chopped
1 c. (2 sticks) BUTTER
1 1/3 c. SUGAR
1/2 c. CORN SYRUP
2 tsp. VANILLA

1. Remove old maids from the popped corn. Put popped corn in a large bowl. Sprinkle pecans and peanuts on top. Do not stir in or they will end up at the bottom.

2. Melt butter. Add sugar and corn syrup. Boil, stirring occasionally, until it turns a light caramel color (about 10 minutes).

3. Remove from heat and add vanilla. Pour over dry ingredients. Stir gently to coat evenly. Spread on a cookie sheet to cool. Store in an air tight container.

4. Yield 1 gallon.

BREAKFASTS

BREAKFAST BURRITOS

5 EGGS
1/2 c. fully cooked HAM, diced
1/2 c. thick and chunky SALSA
1/2 c. CHEDDAR CHEESE, shredded
5 (7-inch) FLOUR TORTILLAS, (Fajita size)

1. Stir together eggs, ham, and salsa in a 12-inch non-stick skillet that has been sprayed with vegetable oil. Scramble until eggs are set.

2. Remove from heat. Stir in cheese. Put 1/3 c. egg mixture on each tortilla and roll up. Place in a 7x11-inch pan that has been sprayed with vegetable oil.

3. Bake, covered, at 350° for 15 minutes. Offer extra salsa.

4. Yield 5 breakfast burritos.

I serve these with BREAKFAST TORTILLAS: make sandwiches by spreading butter and sprinkling cinnamon and sugar between flour tortillas. Stack the sandwiches on top of each other and wrap in foil. Heat through.

BREAKFAST CASSEROLE

1 (5oz.) pkg. CROUTONS, any flavor
2 c. (8oz) SHARP CHEDDAR, shredded
1 lb. SAUSAGE, fried and drained
9 EGGS
1 (12oz.) can EVAPORATED MILK
1 T. MUSTARD

1. Spray a 9x13-inch pan with vegetable oil. Arrange croutons on the bottom.

2. Sprinkle cheese over croutons. Put sausage over cheese.

3. Combine eggs, milk, and mustard. Beat with fork until blended. Pour over ingredients in pan.

4. Bake, covered, at 350° for 45 minutes.

5. Yield 8 servings.

This casserole may be assembled the night before. Cover with foil and store in the refrigerator until morning. Because it serves eight, I like to make it when we have company. Leftovers reheat well. My husband likes to eat it with salsa. But then, he likes to eat everything with salsa!

BREAKFAST PRUNES

2c. (12 oz. pkg.) bite size pitted PRUNES
1 (8 oz.) can or box APPLE JUICE (equals 1 c.)
2 T. HONEY
1/4 tsp. CINNAMON

1. Pour apple juice over prunes. Refrigerate over night.

2. Add honey and cinnamon to prunes and apple juice. Bring to a boil. Reduce heat and simmer, uncovered, for 5 minutes.

3. Serve hot.

4. Yield 2 cups.

Now don't turn up your nose at this recipe or the one on the next page! The prunes are simply delicious, the best I've ever tasted. Leftovers may be kept in the refrigerator and reheated. As for the bananas, they are quite unusual. If you like bananas, you will find them interesting and will probably have found a new and different breakfast side dish. The bananas do not keep and must be eaten immediately.

CARAMEL BANANAS

2 firm BANANAS
2 T. LEMON JUICE
2 T. BUTTER
3 T. HONEY
2 T. BROWN SUGAR

1. Peel bananas and slice in half lengthwise. Cut each of these pieces in half to make 8 pieces total. Dip each piece in lemon juice.

2. Melt the butter, honey, and brown sugar in a 12-inch non-stick skillet. Fry the banana pieces on high turning once. Don't over cook.

3. Serve hot with syrup from skillet poured on top. Offer cinnamon to sprinkle over.

4. Yield 4 servings.

Let all who take refuge in you (Oh, Lord) be glad; let them ever sing for *joy*. Spread your protection over them, that those who love your name may rejoice in you.
Psalm 5:11

MAPLE SYRUP

1 c. WATER
2 c. (1 lb.) BROWN SUGAR
1 tsp. MAPLE BUTTER FLAVORING

1. Bring water and brown sugar to a rapid boil. Boil 3 minutes.
2. Remove from heat and add flavoring.
3. Yield 2 cups.

I buy my flavoring from a company that sells door to door nation wide. If you cannot get it, buy plain maple flavoring from your grocery store.

To make PANCAKES I use a six cup round plastic container with a screw on lid. The opening is large enough to pour into easily and my hand fits easily inside for washing. Pour in 2 cups of a complete pancake mix and mark a line on the outside of the container with a permanent marker. Add 1 3/4 cups of water and mark another line. Screw on the lid and shake well. Adjust the thickness of the batter. I use this container only for pancakes. The lines let me know how much mix and water to add. Remark the lines when they begin to fade. When frying, adjust the heat so the bottom of the pancake will be light brown when the top is full of holes and is starting to look dry. This is the time to flip them.

MONKEY BREAD

2 (7.5 oz.) cans BISCUITS (10 biscuits/can)
1/3 c. SUGAR
2 tsp. CINNAMON
1/4 c. BUTTER
1/3 c. SUGAR

1. Cut biscuits into quarters with scissors. Roll pieces in mixture of 1/3 c. sugar and cinnamon. (May put sugar and cinnamon in a plastic bag and shake pieces to coat.)

2. Arrange pieces in a 7x11-inch pan that has been sprayed with vegetable oil. Sprinkle any extra sugar and cinnamon over the top.

3. Melt butter and 1/3 c. sugar together. Drizzle over biscuit pieces.

4. Bake, uncovered, at 350° for 25 minutes.

Shout with *joy* to God, all the earth! Sing the glory of his name; make his praise glorious! All the earth bows down to you; they sing praise to you, they sing praise to your name.

Psalm 66:1-2,4

PEACH COFFEE CAKE

1 (18oz.) pkg. YELLOW CAKE MIX
1 (21 oz.) can PEACH PIE FILLING
3 EGGS
3 T. SUGAR
1 tsp. CINNAMON

1. Mix together by hand the cake mix, pie filling and eggs.

2. Spread in a 9x13-inch pan that has been sprayed with vegetable oil.

3. Stir together sugar and cinnamon. Sprinkle over cake batter.

4. Bake, uncovered, at 350° for 30 minutes. Test with a toothpick.

5. Yield 8 servings.

This cake is delicious served warm or cold. If I use it as a dessert, I offer whipped topping. To make APPLE COFFEE CAKE: substitute spice cake mix for the yellow cake mix and apple pie filling for the peach pie filling. You may want to cut up the apples a bit.

ROUND UP BREAKFAST

6 strips BACON, diced
1/4 c. ONION, diced
3/4 c. frozen Southern style HASH BROWNS,
    thawed OR diced cooked potatoes
4 EGGS, beaten
3/4 c. (3 oz.) CHEDDAR CHEESE, shredded

1. Fry bacon in a 12-inch non-stick skillet until crisp. Drain on a paper towel.

2. Sauté onion in 2 T. bacon drippings. Add hash browns and fry until brown. Stir in bacon.

3. Pour eggs over mixture in skillet. Lower heat, cover, and cook until eggs are set.

4. Remove from heat. Sprinkle with cheese. Let stand covered, until cheese is melted.

5. Yield 4 servings.

An easy way to dice bacon before it is cooked is to cut it with scissors three strips at a time. Separate the pieces as they cook. If you do not have a lid for your skillet, cover it with foil. The skillet must be large so the eggs will be thin and cook through without turning.

SAUSAGE GRAVY

1 lb. SAUSAGE, fried and drained
1/2 c. FLOUR
3 1/3 c. MILK

1. Sprinkle flour over sausage and mix well.

2. Stir in milk.

3. Heat, stirring constantly, just until it boils. Remove from heat. Adjust seasoning. Serve over biscuits.

4. Yield 4 1/2 cups.

This is my husband's favorite breakfast. I usually fry the sausage at home so it is easy to throw together. I do not like to take much milk camping because of the problem of keeping it cold. I mix 1 c. powdered milk in with the flour and sausage. Then I add 3 1/3 c. water. It tastes just as good.

I either use a large can of biscuits or instant baking mix. For 12 BISQUITS: mix 2 c. baking mix with 2/3 c. milk. Drop from a teaspoon onto a 9x13-inch pan that has been sprayed with vegetable oil. Bake at 400° for 12 minutes. You may mix 1/4 c. powdered milk in with the baking mix and then add 2/3 c. water.

SCOTCH EGGS

4 EGGS, boiled and peeled
1 lb. TURKEY SAUSAGE, my family prefers
    the hot flavored sausage
1 packet from 5 1/2 oz. box CHICKEN
    COATING MIX (shake & bake)

1. Divide sausage into four portions. Flatten into 4-inch circles with damp hands.

2. Cover each boiled egg with a portion of sausage.

3. Roll covered eggs in coating mix. Place in a foil lined 9x13-inch pan that has been sprayed with vegetable oil.

4. Bake, uncovered, at 400° for 30 minutes.

5. Yield 4 Scotch eggs.

This is such a fun and easy recipe. It will certainly impress any RV neighbors you have over for breakfast. Provide steak knives at the table so the little sausage loaves can be cut in half to reveal the egg inside. Add pancakes and you have a gourmet breakfast!

SCRABBLE

4 strips BACON, diced
1/4 c. ONION, chopped
1/2 c. GREEN BELL PEPPER, chopped
1 c. (1 large) TOMATO, seeded and diced
1 (3oz.) pkg. CREAM CHEESE, cubed
1/4 tsp. SALT
6 EGGS, beaten

1. Fry bacon in a 12-inch non-stick skillet until crisp. Place on paper towel to drain.
2. Saute onion and green pepper in 2 T. bacon drippings.
3. Add bacon, tomato, cream cheese, and salt. Cook, stirring constantly until cream cheese is melted.
4. Pour in eggs. Cook, stirring constantly until eggs are set.
5. Yield 5 servings.

SOUPS

CHILI

1 lb. GROUND BEEF, fried and drained
2 (15 oz.) cans CHILI NO BEANS
2 (15 oz.) cans DARK RED KIDNEY BEANS
1 (16 oz.) can TOMATOES, diced

1. Stir all the ingredients together. Do *not* drain the beans or tomatoes.
2. Heat through.
3. Yield 5 cups.

Everyone likes Chili so this is something I make when we have company. I offer soup crackers and shredded cheese to put on top. I also serve okra pickles and sliced cheese.

Hot soup tastes so good when its cold outside. It is perfect to ward off the chill that comes at dusk in the mountains. I also plan to serve soup on our first spring camping trips in Kansas. We get so anxious for that first trip that we have been known to go a little early. One year it even snowed on us.

CREAM OF ASPARAGUS SOUP

1 (11oz.) can condensed CREAM OF
    ASPARAGUS SOUP
1 (8oz.) can cut ASPARAGUS
1/4 c. MILK

1. Stir together soup and liquid from canned asparagus until smooth.

2. Add milk and heat through. Do *not* boil.

3. Cut up asparagus in can with scissors. Add to soup and heat briefly.

4. Yield 2 1/2 cups.

I keep the ingredients for this soup on hand at all times. It is one of my children's favorites. They often fix it for themselves when they are hungry and I have not had time to cook.

The Lord has done great things for us, and we are filled with *joy*.

Psalm 126:3

MINESTRONE

1 (15oz.) can CHILI BEANS
1 (8oz.) can MIXED VEGETABLES
1 (8oz.) can TOMATOES, diced
1 c. WATER
1 BEEF BOUILLON CUBE
25 pieces uncooked SPAGHETTI, broken into
    1" pieces
1/2 lb. fully cooked LITTLE SMOKED
    SAUSAGES, cut into 1/2" pieces

1. Combine all the ingredients. Do *not* drain vegetables.
2. Simmer, covered, until spaghetti is tender.
3. Yield 5 cups.

This Italian soup makes a light meal by itself or serve it with sandwiches. The spicy flavor is a delightful change from the ordinary.

(O Lord), Satisfy us in the morning with your unfailing love, that we may sing for *joy* and be glad all our days.
Psalm 90:14

NEW ENGLAND CLAM CHOWDER

2 medium POTATOES, diced
1 medium ONION, diced
1 c. WATER
1 tsp. SALT
4 slices BACON, fried, drained, and crumbled
3 c. MILK
1 (10 oz.) can WHOLE BABY CLAMS
1 (6 1/2 oz.) can MINCED CLAMS
1/2 c. FLOUR

1. Simmer potatoes and onion in water with salt in a covered pan until tender. Do *not* drain off the water.

2. Add bacon, 2 c. milk, and clams. Do *not* drain the clams. Heat through.

3. Stir the flour into 1 c. milk. Add and heat until thickened. Do *not* boil.

4. Yield 7 cups.

OYSTER BISQUE

1 T. BUTTER
1 (8 oz.) can OYSTER PIECES, do *not* drain
1 tsp. DRIED ONION
1/2 tsp. SALT
1 c. HALF & HALF
1 c. MILK
2 T. FLOUR

1. Melt butter. Add oyster pieces with liquid, dried onion, and salt. Simmer, uncovered, 3 minutes.

2. Add half & half and 2/3 c. milk. Heat until hot, *not* boiling.

3. Stir together 1/3 c. milk and flour with a fork until smooth. Pour slowly into hot mixture. Heat, stirring constantly, to boiling. Remove from heat. Do *not* boil.

4. Yield 3 cups.

Light is shed upon the righteous and *joy* on the upright in heart.

Psalm 97:11

PEPPER SOUP

1 large GREEN BELL PEPPER
1 medium SWEET RED BELL PEPPER
3 c. WATER
3 BEEF BOUILLON CUBES
1/2 tsp. SALT
1/2 lb. GROUND BEEF, fried and drained
1 (8 oz.) can TOMATO SAUCE
1/3 c. INSTANT RICE, uncooked

1. Clean peppers. Cut into 1/2-inch pieces.

2. Add water, bouillon cubes, and salt to peppers. Simmer, covered, until peppers are tender.

3. Add ground beef, tomato sauce, and rice. Cover and simmer until rice is plump.

4. Yield 5 cups.

This soup tastes similar to stuffed peppers. It is very tasty and out of the ordinary. More rice may be added if you like a thicker soup.

Those who sow in tears will reap with songs of *joy*.
Psalm 126:5

POTATO - CORN CHOWDER

4 large POTATOES, diced
1 tsp. SALT
WATER to cover
1 (15 oz.) can CORN, do *not* drain
1 (15 oz.) can CREAM STYLE CORN
1 (12 oz.) can EVAPORATED MILK
1/4 c. INSTANT MASHED POTATO FLAKES

1. Boil potatoes in water with salt in a covered pan until tender.
2. Stir in rest of ingredients.
3. Heat through. Do *not* boil.
4. Yield 8 cups.

This chowder is for hearty appetites. Potatoes and corn are the vegetables we all like. They make a wonderful blend. The instant mashed potato flakes may be left out if your family prefers soup to chowder. Cream soups should never be boiled because they scorch easily. Also, if there is any acidity present, they will curdle.

SALMON CHOWDER

1 (11 oz.) can CONDENSED CREAM OF
    POTATO SOUP
1 (8 oz.) can TOMATOES, diced
1 (5 oz.) can EVAPORATED MILK
1 (6 oz.) can SALMON

1. Drain salmon. Remove skin and bones. Flake.

2. Add other ingredients. Do *not* drain the tomatoes.

3. Heat through. Do *not* boil.

4. Yield 3 cups.

If you like fish chowders, you must try this one. It is so quick and easy to prepare. The ingredients may be kept on hand because they do not require refrigeration.

With *joy* you will draw water from the wells of salvation.
Isaiah 12:3

Rejoice in that day and leap for *joy*, because great is your reward in heaven.
Luke 6:23

SPICY STEW

1 lb. GROUND BEEF, fried and drained
1 SMALL ONION, fried with ground beef
2 (11 oz.) cans CONDENSED VEGETABLE
    BEEF SOUP
1 (10 oz.) can DICED TOMATOES AND
    GREEN CHILIES
1 (11 oz.) can BEEF GRAVY

1. Stir all the ingredients together.

2. Heat through.

3. Yield 7 cups.

My family calls this "Camper Stew" because we often fix it over the camp stove when we first arrive. When you bring the ground beef and onion already fried from home, it is easy for someone to prepare while the others are setting up camp. Add rolls and sliced cheese and you have a very filling meal.

Bring *joy* to your servant, for to you, O Lord; I lift up my soul.

Psalm 86:4

TOMATO BEAN SOUP

1 (11 oz.) can CONDENSED BEAN WITH
    BACON SOUP
1 c. MILK
1 (15 oz.) can STEWED TOMATOES WITH
    ONIONS, CELERY, AND GREEN PEPPERS
1 tsp. CURRY, optional

1. Stir the soup and milk together until smooth.

2. Cut up the tomatoes in the can with scissors. Do *not* drain. Add to soup.

3. Add curry if desired. Heat through. Do *not* boil.

4. Yield 3 1/2 cups.

The curry gives this soup a completely different taste. Try it both ways and see which one you like best. I have not been able to decide. Tomato Bean Soup is very filling. I like to serve corn bread and fresh vegetables to complete the meal.

VEGETABLE SOUP

3 c. WATER
3 BEEF BOUILLON CUBES
1 (15 oz.) can DICED TOMATOES AND
    SWEET ONION, do *not* drain
1 (16 oz.) bag FROZEN MIXED VEGETABLES
1/4 tsp. GARLIC POWDER
1/2 tsp. SALT

1. Combine all the ingredients.

2. Cover and bring to a boil. Reduce
    heat and simmer for 25 minutes.

3. Yield 5 1/2 cups.

If you want more broth in your soup, add another cup of
water and another beef bouillon cube. To make
VEGETABLE BEEF SOUP, add 1/2 lb. of ground beef
that has been fried and drained. You may also add 1/2
cup of uncooked small shell pasta.

Do not cast me from your presence or take your Holy
Spirit from me. Restore to me the *joy* of your salvation
and grant me a willing spirit, to sustain me.
                                                    Psalm 51:11-12

SANDWICHES

HAM AND SWISS MELTS

1 (6 oz.) pkg. thin sliced DELI HAM
6 slices SWISS CHEESE
1 (7 oz.) can SLICED MUSHROOMS, drained
6 HAMBURGER BUNS
BUTTER

1. Split buns in half and butter lightly.

2. Divide ham, cheese, and mushrooms and layer on bottom buns. Put on bun tops.

3. Wrap in foil and bake at 350° for 10 minutes.

4. Yield 6 sandwiches.

You may make these ahead and refrigerate. They keep well for a couple days. Because they are cold, add five minutes on to the baking time. You may wrap them in paper towels and heat them in a microwave if you have one. Be careful not to leave them in too long. A microwave can ruin bread in a hurry.

God has set you above your companions by anointing you with the oil of *joy*.

Hebrews 1:9

HOT CLUCKERS

1 (5 oz.) jar OLD ENGLISH PASTEURIZED
    PROCESS CHEESE SPREAD
1 (5 oz.) can CHUNK CHICKEN, drained
1/4 c. GREEN OLIVES, chopped
2 T. ONION, diced
4 FRENCH HARD ROLLS, split lengthwise
BUTTER

1. Lightly butter hard roll halves.

2. Combine cheese spread, chicken, olives,
   and onion. Spread on bottom rolls. Put on
   roll tops.

3. Wrap in foil and bake at 350° for 10 minutes.

4. Yield 4 sandwiches.

Don't tell anyone about the olives and they'll never know!
They add a wonderful salty flavor. You may eat this
sandwich hot or cold. Refer to page 48 for tips on
making the day before or using a microwave. Camping
calls for a lot of sandwiches. I like to get out of the
hot dog/hamburger/ham sandwich routine.

MEXICAN SANDWICH SPREAD

1 (5 oz.) can CHUNK HAM
1 (4.5 oz.) can CHOPPED GREEN CHILIES,
    drained
1 c. finely shredded MONTEREY JACK CHEESE
1 tsp. HOT PEPPER SAUCE
1 large TOMATO
LETTUCE
4 KAISER ROLLS

1. Cut rolls in half and butter lightly.

2. Combine deviled ham, chilies, cheese, and hot pepper sauce. Hot pepper sauce may be doubled if preferred.

3. Spread filling on roll bottoms. Top with tomato slice and lettuce. Put on roll tops.

4. Serve hot. Heating directions are on page 48. Add tomato and lettuce after heating.

5. Yield 4 sandwiches.

ONION BAGELWICHES

4 ONION BAGELS, split
1 (6 oz.) pkg. thin sliced DELI TURKEY
    BREAST
1 (6 oz.) pkg. sliced PROVOLONE CHEESE
1 large TOMATO, sliced
LETTUCE

1. Divide turkey between 4 bagel bottoms. Top with cheese slices.

2. Place all 8 bagel halves on a foil covered oven rack. Bake, uncovered, at 350° for 10 minutes.

3. Put tomato slice, lettuce, and extra bagel half on top of melted cheese.

4. Yield 4 sandwiches.

I offer mayonnaise, mustard, and horseradish sauce with these sandwiches. Other deli meats may be used instead of or in addition to the turkey. I make one per person as they are quite filling.

My lips will shout for *joy* when I sing praise to you—I, whom you have redeemed.

Psalm 71:23

PEPPERONI CALZONES

8 (7-inch) FLOUR TORTILLAS, (Fajita size)
1 c. PIZZA SAUCE
8 tsp. PARMESAN CHEESE
1 c. RICOTTA CHEESE
48 slices (2.5 oz. pkg.) PEPPERONI
1 c. MOZZARELLA CHEESE, shredded

1. Spread 2 T. pizza sauce on each tortilla. Sprinkle with 2 t. Parmesan cheese.

2. Place 2 T. ricotta on top half of tortilla. Arrange 6 slices pepperoni on top of ricotta. Sprinkle 2 T. mozzarella on top of pepperoni.

3. Fold bottom half of tortilla over filled top half.

4. Place calzones on a foil covered oven rack. Bake, uncovered, at 350° for 10 minutes.

5. Yield 8 sandwiches.

Ground beef, ham, or shrimp may be used instead of pepperoni. Onions, olives, green peppers, or mushrooms may also be added, but do not overfill. I plan two sandwiches per person.

PIMIENTO CHEESE SPREAD

1 (5 oz.) jar OLD ENGLISH PASTEURIZED
    PROCESS CHEESE SPREAD
1 (8 oz.) pkg. shredded PASTEURIZED
    PROCESS CHEESE
1 (2 oz.) jar DICED PIMIENTOS, drained
1/4 c. MAYONNAISE
1 T. MILK
4 HARD BOILED EGGS, chopped

1. Beat together cheese spread, shredded cheese, pimientos, mayonnaise, and milk.

2. Add chopped eggs. Keep refrigerated. Serve cold for sandwich spread.

3. Yield 2 3/4 cups spread or 11 sandwiches.

This Pimiento Cheese Spread tastes better and costs less than what you can buy ready made in the store. It is great to have ready for a snack when the kids come in hungry. I boil extra eggs so I can also make EGG SALAD: 4 chopped hard boiled eggs, 1/4 c. mayonnaise, 1/8 t. salt will make 4 egg salad sandwiches.

PITA FAJITAS

1/2 lb. LEAN PORK, thinly sliced
1/2 c. ITALIAN SALAD DRESSING
1 AVOCADO, peeled and sliced
1 T. LEMON JUICE
1/4 c. SOUR CREAM
1/4 c. thick and chunky SALSA
1/2 c. CHEDDAR CHEESE, shredded
2 loaves PITA BREAD

1. Marinate pork in salad dressing one hour or more. Drain excess dressing. Fry in a 12-inch non-stick skillet until liquid is evaporated. Drain grease, if any.

2. Sprinkle avocado slices with lemon juice.

3. Cut pita bread loaves in half. Open to form pockets. Fill with pork, avocado, 1 T. sour cream, 1 T. salsa, and 2 T. cheese.

4. Yield 4 sandwiches.

Chicken or beef may be used instead of pork and lettuce may be used instead of avocado. You'll love Pita Fajitas!

REUBEN SANDWICHES

12 slices RYE BREAD
BUTTER
THOUSAND ISLAND SALAD DRESSING
1 (6 oz.) pkg. thin sliced DELI CORNED BEEF
1 (8 oz.) can SAUERKRAUT, drained
6 slices SWISS CHEESE

1. Lightly butter both sides of all 12 slices of bread.
2. Spread 1 tsp. dressing on one side of all 12 slices of bread.
3. Place corned beef on 6 slices. Top with sauerkraut and Swiss cheese. Put on other 6 slices, dressing side down.
4. Fry 3 at a time in a 12-inch non-stick skillet until sides are crisp and brown.
5. Yield 6 sandwiches.

Ask and you will receive, and your *joy* will be complete.
John 16:24

SLOPPY BEEF BURGERS

1 lb. GROUND BEEF, fried and drained
1 (11 oz.) can condensed FIESTA CHILI BEEF
    WITH BEANS SOUP
1/2 c. WATER
8 HAMBURGER BUNS

1. Combine ground beef, soup, and water.

2. Heat, stirring constantly, until very hot.

3. Use a rounded 1/3 cup beef filling for each bun.

4. Yield 3 cups or 8 sandwiches.

Try this sandwich as an alternative to the customary grilled hamburger. It is very tasty plain, but you may offer the usual condiments that are eaten on hot dogs and hamburgers—diced onions, tomatoes, lettuce, cheese slices, dill pickles, mustard, and ketchup.

Shout aloud and sing for *joy*, people of Zion, for great is the Holy One of Israel among you.

                                                Isaiah 12:6

SALADS

AMBROSIA

1 (15 oz.) can PINEAPPLE TIDBITS
1 (11 oz.) can MANDARIN ORANGES
1 c. COCONUT
1 c. SOUR CREAM
1 c. MINIATURE MARSHMALLOWS

1. Drain fruit well. Combine with coconut and sour cream. Fold in marshmallows before serving.
2. Yield 4 cups.

Ambrosia is so luscious it could easily be served as a light dessert. If you prefer the marshmallows to be soft and a bit melted, add them several hours before serving.

My grandmother served some sort of salad at every meal. She did not think a meal was complete without one. I know with our limited time we are often doing well just to get a main dish served. The recipes in this salad section are quick and easy to make. They also keep well in the refrigerator so may be pulled out to rapidly "complete" our hurried meals. Grandma would have liked them.

APPLESAUCE SALAD

1 large or 2 small boxes GELATIN
2 c. BOILING WATER
1 (16 oz.) can APPLESAUCE

1. Stir gelatin and boiling water together in a 4 c. container until gelatin is dissolved.

2. Stir in applesauce. Seal and chill until set.

3. Yield 4 cups.

Applesauce Salad is always refreshing on a hot summer's day. This recipe makes a gelatin salad that is more solid than most and can be eaten with a fork. It will not melt as easily on a warm plate or on hot days.

The applesauce may be replaced by any 16 oz. can of fruit. Do not drain off the juice. I like to match the fruit to the gelatin flavor. From Bing cherry to pineapple, the varieties are endless. I do not like the canned strawberries or raspberries, so I use a 16 oz. frozen container of these berries. Do not drain off the syrup.

To make RED HOT APPLESAUCE SALAD: use red gelatin and simmer 1 c. red hot candies in the water until melted.

FRUIT SALAD

1 (11 oz.) can MANDARIN ORANGES
1 (16 oz.) can CHUNKY MIXED FRUIT
1 c. FRUIT JUICE
1 small pkg. INSTANT VANILLA PUDDING

1. Drain fruit, reserving 1 cup juice.
2. Combine fruit juice and pudding mix. Beat with wire whisk until smooth.
3. Stir in fruit. Chill.
4. Yield 3 cups.

Be sure to use a wire whisk to avoid lumps. Try making this salad by using other combinations, such as 1 (15 oz.) can chunk pineapple, 1 (15 oz.) can tropical fruit, and instant lemon pudding, or 2 (17 oz.) cans fruit cocktail and instant white chocolate pudding. You may toss in some fresh fruit such as sliced bananas or grapes.

God has ascended amid shouts of *joy*, the Lord amid the sounding of trumpets. Sing praises to God, sing praises; sing praises to our King, sing praises.

Psalm 47:5-6

GLORIFIED RICE

3/4 c. INSTANT RICE, uncooked
3/4 c. BOILING WATER
1 (8 oz.) can CRUSHED PINEAPPLE, drained
1 1/2 c. (4 oz.) FROZEN WHIPPED
    TOPPING, thawed
1 c. MINIATURE MARSHMALLOWS

1. Stir rice and water together. Cover and let set 10 minutes.

2. Stir in pineapple, whipped topping, and marshmallows. Cover and chill.

3. Yield 3 cups.

Use fat-free whipped topping and you have a rich tasting salad that is totally fat-free. The rice will absorb more liquid as it sets. Add a little milk if the salad seems too dry.

Let the fields be jubilant, and everything in them. Then all the trees of the forest will sing for *joy*.
                                        Psalm 96:12

ORANGE FLUFF

1 1/2 c. COTTAGE CHEESE
1 small pkg. ORANGE GELATIN, dry
1 1/2 c. (4 oz.) FROZEN WHIPPED TOPPING,
   thawed
1 (11 oz.) can MANDARIN ORANGES, drained
1 (15 oz.) can CRUSHED PINEAPPLE, drained

1. Combine cottage cheese, gelatin, and whipped topping.

2. Fold in mandarin oranges and pineapple.

3. Yield 5 cups.

This salad may be made by leaving out the mandarin oranges and pineapple. Any flavor of gelatin may be used for this variation. It is an easy way to add a bright color and a delightful flavor to a meal.

Your dead will live; their bodies will rise. You who dwell in the dust, wake up and shout for *joy*.

Isaiah 26:19

PEA SALAD

1 (10 oz.) box frozen peas, thawed and
   drained
1 hard boiled EGG, chopped
1/2 c. shredded MILD CHEDDAR CHEESE
1/4 c. MAYONNAISE
1 tsp. SUGAR
1/4 tsp. SALT

1. Combine peas, egg, and cheese.

2. Stir together mayonnaise, sugar, and salt. Fold
   into pea mixture.

3. Yield 2 1/2 cups.

This is a delicious basic pea salad recipe. I like it as is,
but you may add any of your favorite extra ingredients,
such as crumbled bacon, diced onion, chopped celery,
shredded carrots, chopped water chestnuts, or raisins.

I (the Lord) will turn their mourning into gladness; I will
give them comfort and *joy* instead of sorrow.

Jeremiah 31:13

PICKLED BEANS

1 small SWEET ONION, sliced thin
2 (14 oz.) cans GREEN BEANS, drain and save
   juice
BEAN JUICE
1/2 c. VINEGAR
1/4 c. OIL
1/2 c. SUGAR
1/4 tsp. SALT

1. Separate onion slices into rings. Combine
   with green beans.
2. Stir together bean juice, vinegar, oil, sugar, and
   salt. Heat, stirring, until sugar and salt are
   dissolved. Pour over green beans and onions.
3. Chill and marinate 2 hours.
4. Yield 4 cups.

Shout for *joy*, O heavens; rejoice, O earth; burst into
song, O mountains! For the Lord comforts his people
and will have compassion on his afflicted ones.
Isaiah 49:13

64

VEGETABLES

APPLE-YAMS

1 (40 oz.) can cut YAMS, drained
1 tsp. MAPLE FLAVORING
1 (25 oz.) can CHUNKY APPLESAUCE
1/2 c. BROWN SUGAR
1 tsp. CINNAMON

1. Smash yams with a fork. Yams will not be totally smooth, but a little chunky. Stir in maple flavoring. Pour into a 7x11-inch pan that has been sprayed with vegetable oil.

2. Drain applesauce if there is much liquid. Stir together applesauce, brown sugar, and cinnamon. Pour on top of yams.

3. Bake, uncovered, at 375° for 30 minutes.

4. Yield 6 servings.

These Apple-Yams are so delicious. The two flavors compliment each other perfectly. I often serve them with grilled chops or steaks instead of baked potatoes.

At his tabernacle will I sacrifice with shouts of *joy*; I will sing and make music to the Lord.

Psalm 27:6

CHEESY TOT CASSEROLE

1 (11 oz.) can CONDENSED CHEDDAR
    CHEESE SOUP
1 (12 oz.) can EVAPORATED MILK
1 c. SOUR CREAM
1 tsp. GARLIC POWDER
1 (32 oz.) bag FROZEN TATER TOTS
2 c. (8 oz.) CHEDDAR CHEESE, shredded

1. Stir together soup, milk, sour cream and garlic powder.

2. Gently stir in frozen tater tots.

3. Pour into a 9x13-inch pan that has been sprayed with vegetable oil.

4. Sprinkle cheese on top.

5. Bake, uncovered, at 350° for 50 minutes.

6. Yield 10 servings.

Take this casserole to a carry in dinner at an RV park and you will get many compliments. Aren't those dinners fun?

67

ESCALLOPED CORN

1 (10 oz.) box FROZEN CORN
1 tsp. DRIED ONION
1/2 tsp. SALT
1/4 c. WATER
1 (5 oz.) can EVAPORATED MILK
2 tsp. CORN STARCH

1. Combine corn, onion, salt, and water. Simmer, covered, until corn is tender.

2. Stir together milk and corn starch. Add to corn. Heat, stirring constantly, until thickened.

3. Yield 2 cups or 4 servings.

Everyone likes corn and Escalloped Corn is especially delicious. If I have access to half and half I will use it in place of the evaporated milk. Now, I know it is not as healthy, but I like to splurge occasionally.

I (Jesus) will see you again and you will rejoice, and no one will take away your *joy*.

John 16:22

HARVARD BEETS

1/3 c. BEET JUICE
1 1/2 tsp. CORN STARCH
1 T. SUGAR
1 T. VINEGAR
sprinkle SALT
1 (15 oz.) can SLICED BEETS, drained

1. Combine beet juice, corn starch, sugar, vinegar, and salt. Add sliced beets.

2. Heat, stirring constantly, until thickened and clear.

3. Yield 1 1/2 cups.

A variation of this recipe is to replace the sugar and vinegar with 2 T. orange breakfast drink powder to make delicious ORANGE GLAZED BEETS.

Praise the Lord with the harp; make music to him on the ten-stringed lyre. Sing to him a new song; play skillfully, and shout for *joy*.

Psalm 33:2-3

ONION RICE

1/4 c. (1/2 stick) BUTTER
1 MEDUIM ONION, diced
1 (10 1/2 oz.) can FRENCH ONION SOUP
1 c. WATER
2 c. INSTANT RICE, uncooked

1. Sauté onion in butter until onion is tender.

2. Add soup and water. Bring to a boil.

3. Remove from heat. Stir in rice. Cover and let set 5 minutes. Fluff with a fork. If there is still a little liquid, simmer and stir until it is absorbed.

4. Yield 4 1/2 cups.

Onion Rice is a wonderful, light accompaniment to a main dish. I use leftover rice in many ways. It is good added to soup. It may also be added to meat and vegetable leftovers with a can of gravy to make a casserole.

The kingdom of God is not a matter of eating and drinking, but of righteousness, peace and *joy* in the Holy Spirit.
Romans 14:17

SKILLET SQUASH

1 (8 oz.) can TOMATOES, diced, do *not* drain
1/2 c. ONION, chopped
2 c. (1 med.) ZUCCHINI, peeled and sliced
    1/4-inch thick
1/4 tsp. SALT

1. Stir together ingredients in a 12-inch non-stick skillet. Cover and simmer until squash is tender. Add very little water if needed.

2. Uncover and cook until liquid is evaporated.

3. Yield 1 1/2 cups or 3 servings.

We like all kinds of squash fixed in every way you can think of. And if you grow squash, you know you better like it because it usually produces more than you can eat or give away. Zucchini should be tender enough to insert a fingernail in the skin. Large zucchini that have become hard will need to be seeded. When we go camping, we take zucchini and hang it in a tree to keep the squirrels and rodents from helping themselves. We also store onions, potatoes and some fruits this way. Of course, you can't do this in bear country. It is nice to have some fresh food when you are camping. If you don't have a lid for your skillet, set the 9x13-inch pan on top. It won't completely cover, but will suffice.

ZIPPY GLAZED CARROTS

1 T. BUTTER
1 T. BROWN SUGAR
1 tsp. MUSTARD
1/4 tsp. SALT
1 (15 oz.) can SLICED CARROTS, drained

1. Combine butter, brown sugar, mustard, and salt in a 12-inch non-stick skillet. Cook until blended.
2. Add carrots. Fry until carrots are heated and glazed.
3. Yield 1 1/2 cups or 4 servings.

No one will know that you did not take the time to peel, slice, and cook these delicious carrots. Everyone will love the zippy flavor. Our family only ate carrots in stew or pot roast until I found this recipe.

May the nations be glad and sing for *joy*, for you rule the peoples justly and guide the nations of the earth.
Paslm 67:4

MAIN DISHES

BRATWURST BAKE

1 lb. fully cooked SMOKED BRATWURST, cut into 1/4-inch slices
1 large ONION, diced
4 med. POTATOES, peel, cut lengthwise, then into 1/4-inch slices
1/2 c. FLOUR
1 (11 oz.) can CONDENSED CREAM OF CELERY SOUP
1 c. MILK

1. Toss together bratwurst, onion, potatoes, and flour in a 9x13-inch pan that has been sprayed with vegetable oil.

2. Stir together celery soup and milk. Pour over other ingredients.

3. Bake, covered, at 375° for 1 hour.

4. Yield 6 servings.

Where morning dawns and evening fades you, (O Lord), call forth songs of *joy*.

Psalm 65:8

CHEESY CHICKEN BUNDLES

1 (11 oz.) can CONDENSED CREAM OF
    CHICKEN SOUP
1/2 c. MILK
3/4 c. PASTEURIZED PROCESS CHEESE,
    shredded or cubed
1 (10 oz.) can CHUNK CHICKEN, drained and
    flaked
1 (8 oz.) can CRESCENT ROLLS

1. Combine soup, milk, and cheese. Heat until melted and smooth. Pour into a 7x11-inch pan that has been sprayed with vegetable oil.

2. Separate crescents into 8 triangles. Place 2 T. chicken on wide end of crescent and roll. Pinch to seal. Place on top of sauce.

3. Bake, uncovered, at 375° for 25 minutes until golden brown. Serve with sauce on top.

4. Yield 8 chicken bundles or 4 servings.

CHICKEN POT PIE

2 (9-inch) deep dish frozen PIE SHELLS
1 (10 oz.) can CHUNK CHICKEN, drained
1 (15 oz.) can MIXED VEGETABLES, drained
1 (2.8 oz.) can FRENCH FRIED ONION
    RINGS
2 (11 oz.) cans CONDENSED CREAM OF
    CHICKEN SOUP
1/4 tsp. SALT

1. Prick bottom pie shell all over with fork. Bake, uncovered, at 375° for 10 minutes.

2. Combine chicken, vegetables, onion rings, soup, and salt. Fill bottom pie shell with mixture.

3. Place second pie shell on top. Prick with fork 6 places. Set on a foil covered oven rack to catch spills. Bake, uncovered, at 375° for 40 minutes.

4. Yield 6 servings.

How wonderful! Chicken pot pie you can make without deboning a chicken and peeling vegetables. It has the convenience of boughten pot pies, but tastes so much better.

CHILI PIE

1 lb. GROUND BEEF, fried and drained
1 (15 oz.) can CHILI WITH BEANS
1 (15 oz.) can CHILI NO BEANS
1 (10.5 oz.) pkg. CORN CHIPS
TOPPINGS

1. Combine ground beef and chili. Heat through.

2. To serve, place a handful of corn chips in bottom of bowl. Top with chili mixture.

3. Offer toppings such as shredded cheese, diced onions, sour cream, mustard, ketchup, lettuce, tomatoes, and avocados.

4. Yield 4 servings.

Chili Pie has got to be one of my family's favorites. It takes almost no time to prepare, especially if the ground beef is already cooked.

You will go out in *joy* and be led forth in peace; the mountains and hills will burst into song before you, and all the trees of the field will clap their hands.
Isaiah 55:12

CHINESE EGG ROLLS

1 lb. GROUND PORK, fried and drained
2 (14 oz.) cans FANCY MIXED CHINESE
      VEGETABLES, drained
1 (16 oz.) pkg. WONTON WRAPPERS (16
      wrappers)
1 c. SHORTENING
DIPPING SAUCE

1. Combine pork and vegetables.

2. Place 1/3 cup mixture on each wrapper. Roll,
   folding in ends according to package directions.

3. Heat shortening in a 12-inch non-stick skillet.
   Cooking 8 at a time, fry each side until brown.
   Drain on paper towels. Serve with your favorite
   dipping sauce.

4. Yield 16 Chinese egg rolls or 5 servings.

Finally, egg rolls without the work of preparing cabbage
and other vegetables. My family likes boughten sweet
and sour sauce for dipping and a side dish of rice.

CHUCKWAGON SQUARES

1 (10 oz.) can PIZZA DOUGH
1 lb. GROUND BEEF, fried and drained
1 (16 oz.) can PORK AND BEANS, drained
1/2 c. chopped ONION
1/2 c. KETCHUP
1 T. MUSTARD
1/2 tsp. SALT
3/4 c. CHEDDAR CHEESE, shredded

1. Unroll pizza dough and press in a 9x13-inch pan that has been sprayed with vegetable oil.

2. Combine ground beef, pork and beans, onion, ketchup, mustard, and salt. Spread on top of dough. Sprinkle with cheese.

3. Bake, uncovered, at 400° for 25 minutes. Let set 5 minutes before serving.

4. Yield 6 servings.

GREEN CHILE CHICKEN

6 CHICKEN BREASTS, boneless and skinless
1 (4.5 oz.) can CHOPPED GREEN CHILIES, do
    not drain
1 (11 oz.) can CONDENSED CREAM OF
    CHICKEN SOUP
1 c. MONTEREY JACK CHEESE, shredded

1. Wash chicken and pat dry. Place in a
   7x11-inch pan that has been sprayed with
   vegetable oil.

2. Stir together chilies and soup. Spoon over
   chicken.

3. Bake, uncovered, at 350° for 50 minutes.
   Remove from oven and sprinkle cheese on top.
   Bake 10 minutes longer.

4. Yield 6 servings.

   You may make Green Chile Chicken in a 12-inch non-stick
   skillet. Spray the skillet well with vegetable oil.
   Simmer the chicken breasts, covered, until tender. Pour
   over the sauce and simmer, covered, until hot and thick.
   Sprinkle on the cheese and cover until melted.

QUICHE

1 (9-inch) deep dish FROZEN PIE SHELL, uncooked
1/2 lb. BACON, fried, drained, and crumbled
3/4 c. CHEDDAR CHEESE, shredded
1 (12 oz.) can EVAPORATED MILK
3 EGGS

1. Sprinkle bacon over bottom of pie shell.

2. Sprinkle cheese on top of bacon.

3. Beat eggs and milk together by hand. Pour over bacon and cheese.

4. Bake, uncovered, at 375° for 40 minutes. Knife should come out clean when inserted.

5. Yield 6 servings.

Send forth your light and your truth, let them guide me; let them bring me to your holy mountain, to the place where you dwell. Then will I go to the altar of God, to God, my *joy* and my delight. I will praise you with the harp, O God, my God.

Psalm 43:3-4

81

RAPID RICE DINNER

1 c. BOILING WATER
1 c. INSTANT RICE, uncooked
2 T. BUTTER
1/2 c. CELERY, chopped
1/4 c. ONION, diced
1 (6 oz.) bag FROZEN SALAD SHRIMP
1 (11 oz.) can condensed NEW ENGLAND
    CLAM CHOWDER
1/2 c. SOUR CREAM
1/4 tsp. SALT
1/4 tsp. CURRY, optional

1. Add rice to boiling water. Cover and set aside.

2. Sauté celery and onion in butter. Rinse shrimp in cold water. Drain on paper towel. Add to celery and onion. Heat through.

3. Add soup, sour cream, salt, curry, and rice. Heat, stirring constantly.

4. Yield 3 1/2 cups or 4 servings

SALMON PATTIES

1 (14 oz.) can SALMON, drained
1/2 c. CRACKERS, crushed
4 tsp. DRIED ONION
2 EGGS
1/2 c. SHORTENING

1. Combine all the ingredients except shortening. Form into five 1/2-inch thick patties.

2. Heat shortening in a 12-inch non-stick skillet. Fry each side until brown. Drain on paper towels.

3. Yield 5 patties.

I offer several different sauces when I fix Salmon Patties. The members of my family have different tastes. Try lemon juice, tartar sauce, or sea food sauce. My daughter combines ketchup and horseradish, while my husband mixes mayonnaise and ketchup. I like to pour creamed peas over the top of mine. My college cafeteria always offered them this way. They are delicious no matter how you serve them—even plain!

SIMPLE TUNA CASSEROLE

1 (7 oz.) can SHOESTRING POTATOES,
    found by the potato chips
1 (12 oz.) can TUNA, drained and flaked
1 (7 oz.) can MUSHROOM PIECES, do *not*
    drain
1 (12 oz.) can EVAPORATED MILK
2 (11 oz.) cans CONDENSED CREAM OF
    MUSHROOM SOUP
1 (6 oz.) pkg. PROVOLONE CHEESE SLICES

1. Stir together the shoestring potatoes,
   tuna, mushrooms, milk, and soup. Pour into
   a 9x13-inch pan that has been sprayed
   with vegetable oil. Place cheese on top.

2. Bake, covered, at 350° for 45 minutes.

3. Yield 8 servings.

My Lord is my strength and my shield; my heart trusts
in him, and I am helped. My heart leaps for *joy* and I
will give thanks to him in song.

Psalm 28:7

SPAGHETTI

1 1/2 lb. GROUND BEEF, fried and drained
2 1/2 c. WATER
1 (26 oz.) can SPAGHETTI SAUCE
5 oz. SPAGHETTI, (1-inch diameter handful)

1. Add water and spaghetti sauce to ground beef. Bring to a boil.

2. Break spaghetti into thirds and stir in. It will stick straight up. Leave it, do not break it more.

3. Cover and simmer, stirring occasionally, for 30 minutes. Spaghetti will soon become tender and stir in.

4. Yield 7 cups or 7 servings.

This Spaghetti is not fancy, but it tastes good and is so much easier than cooking and draining the spaghetti in a separate pan. Serve it with tossed salad and bread sticks and your family will rave about their wonderful meal.

The father of a righteous man has great *joy*; he who has a wise son delights in him.

Proverbs 23:24

STROGANOFF

1 lb. GROUND BEEF, fried and drained
4 c. WATER
2 T. DRIED ONION
1 tsp. SALT
3 c. (6 oz.) WIDE EGG NOODLES, uncooked
1 (11 oz.) can CONDENSED CREAM OF
     MUSHROOM SOUP
1 (3 oz.) pkg. CREAM CHEESE
1 (10 oz.) box FROZEN CORN, opt.

1. Combine ground beef, water, dried onion, and salt. Bring to a boil.

2. Stir in noodles, soup, and cream cheese. Cover and simmer 20 minutes, stirring occasionally.

3. Uncover, add corn if desired, and cook until thick.

4. Yield 8 cups.

This Stroganoff is so good and so easy. It will serve five or six depending on what you serve with it. Canned corn, drained, may be used in place of the frozen corn.

STUFFED POTATOES

1 (10 oz.) box FROZEN CHOPPED BROCCOLI
1/4 c. WATER
1 (1lb.) pkg. fully cooked HAM, julienne strips,
    usually found in the grocery salad section
1 (8 oz.) jar PASTEURIZED PROCESS
    CHEESE SAUCE
6 large BAKED POTATOES

1. Simmer broccoli in water until tender.
   Keep pan covered.

2. Add ham and cheese sauce. Heat through.

3. Split hot, baked potatoes open and stuff
   with broccoli mixture.

4. Yield 4 cups or 6 stuffed potatoes.

I offer butter and sour cream as additional toppings.
Stuffed Potatoes are very filling. A salad and bread are
all that are needed to complete the meal.

The meadows are covered with flocks and the valleys
are mantled with grain; they shout for *joy* and sing.
                                          Psalm 65:13

TURKEY DRESSING CASSEROLE

1 (6 serving) box INSTANT CHICKEN
    FLAVOR STUFFING MIX
3 (5 oz.) cans CHUNK TURKEY, drained
1 c. MILD CHEDDAR CHEESE, shredded
1 (11 oz.) can CONDENSED CREAM OF
    CHICKEN SOUP
1/3 c. MILK
1 (10 oz.) can TURKEY GRAVY

1. Make stuffing according to package directions.
   Put stuffing in a 7x11-inch pan that has been
   sprayed with vegetable oil. Flake turkey and
   put on top of dressing. Sprinkle with cheese.

2. Stir together soup, milk, and gravy. Pour over
   turkey.

3. Bake, covered, at 350° for 40 minutes.

4. Yield 6 servings.

A cheerful look brings *joy* to the heart, and good news
gives health to the bones.

Proverbs 15:30

BREADS

BLUE CHEESE PINWHEELS

1 (8 oz.) can CRESCENT ROLLS
4 T. (1/4 c.) CHUNKY BLUE CHEESE
    SALAD DRESSING

1. Separate crescent rolls into two
   rectangles. Press to seal perforations.

2. Spread 2 T, dressing over each rectangle.
   Gently roll up each rectangle loosely so the
   dressing does not squish out.

3. Carefully cut each roll into 4 pieces with a sharp
   serrated knife. Place in a foil lined 9x13-inch
   pan that has been sprayed with vegetable oil.

4. Bake, uncovered, at 400° for 15 minutes.
   Pinwheels should be golden brown.

6. Yield 8 pinwheels.

If you want a stronger blue cheese flavor you may add
some crumbled blue cheese to the salad dressing. This
is a delicious and unsual bread.

BREAD STICKS

4 HOT DOG BUNS
6 T. BUTTER
1/2 tsp. GARLIC POWDER
2 T. PARMESAN CHEESE

1. Split buns in half. Cut each piece in half lengthwise to make 16 sticks.

2. Melt butter in a non-stick 12-inch skillet. Dip cut sides of buns in butter. Place butter-side up in an ungreased, foil lined, 9x13-inch pan.

3. Sprinkle with garlic powder and cheese.

4. Bake, uncovered, at 250° for 1 hour.

5. Yield 16 bread sticks.

These Bread Sticks are wonderful with spaghetti and salad. They are crunchy like croutons. Return them to the oven to make crisper, if needed.

By using a 12-inch skillet, the melted butter will be shallow and the bread will not soak up as much. Try replacing the garlic powder with either seasoned salt or dill weed. We like both variations.

FANCY FRENCH ROLLS

4 FRENCH HARD ROLLS
BUTTER
1 c. SHREDDED COLBY/MONTEREY JACK
　　CHEESE BLEND

1. Split hard rolls lengthwise. Butter each half.

2. Place 8 roll halves, butter side up, on a foil covered oven rack. Sprinkle 2 T. cheese on top of each roll.

3. Bake, uncovered, at 350° for 10 minutes.

4. Yield 8 rolls.

These rolls are crisp on the outside with a soft, cheesy top. They are delicious. Colby and Monterey Jack cheeses may be bought already blended. They have a mild flavor that goes well with spicy food. Try this recipe with some of the seasoned cheese blends to add flavor to an otherwise plain meal. I want to thank my sister, who gave me this recipe. She is a great cook.

You will find your *joy* in the Lord.

Isaiah 58:14

HERBED ROLLS

1 (3 oz.) pkg. CREAM CHEESE
2 T. BUTTER
1 tsp. dried ITALIAN HERB SEASONING
    BLEND
1 doz. BROWN 'N SERVE ROLLS

1. Stir together cream cheese, butter, and herbs until smooth.

2. Split each roll about half way. Do not pull completely apart. Spread 1 1/2 teaspoonfuls of cheese mixture in each roll.

3. Place rolls on a foil covered oven rack. Bake, uncovered, at 375° for 8 minutes.

4. Yield 12 rolls.

I have used other dried herbs instead of the Italian blend. Each herb has it's own unique flavor. Parsley flakes, chives, dill weed, majoram—try your own favorite.

Your statutes (O Lord), are my heritage forever; they are the *joy* of my heart.

Psalm 119:111

NUTTY BREAD

2 c. INSTANT BAKING MIX
2/3 c. DRY ROASTED SUNFLOWER
    KERNELS, divided
1/3 c. BROWN SUGAR
2/3 c. CREAMY PEANUT BUTTER
1 c. MILK

1. Stir together baking mix, 1/3 c. sunflower kernels, brown sugar, peanut butter, and milk.

2. Turn into a 7x11-inch pan that has been sprayed with vegetable oil. Spread flat.

3. Sprinkle 1/3 c. sunflower kernels on top. Gently press down so they will stick to batter.

4. Bake, uncovered, at 375° for 20 minutes.

This delicious, earthy bread goes well with grilled or baked chicken. We like it served warm or cold.

Do not grieve, for the *joy* of the Lord is your strength.
Nehemiah 8:10

QUESADILLAS

1 (3 oz.) pkg. CREAM CHEESE
1 c. (4 oz.) MONTEREY JACK CHEESE,
    shredded
1 (4 oz.) can CHOPPED GREEN CHILIES,
    drained
4 (7-inch) FLOUR TORTILLAS, (Fajita size)
1/4 c. OIL

1. Combine cream cheese, Monterey Jack cheese and green chilies. Spread over 4 tortillas.

2. Heat oil in a 12-inch non-stick skillet.

3. Fold tortillas in half and fry 2 at a time until each side is brown and crisp. Drain on paper towels.

4. Yield 4 quesadillas.

Try using chopped jalapeños instead of the green chilies. I serve this bread with grilled steak or pork chops to add a Mexican touch to the meal. The Quesadillas may be wrapped in foil and heated in the oven or placed on the grill, if you do not want to fry them.

SKILLET CORN CAKES

1 c. CORNMEAL
1 c. INSTANT BAKING MIX
1 tsp. SALT
1 (15 oz.) can CORN, do *not* drain
1/4 c. (1/2 stick) BUTTER

1. Stir together cornmeal, baking mix, and salt.

2. Stir in corn and liquid.

3. Heat butter in a 12-inch non-stick skillet. Use 1/4 c. batter and make a thin patty. Fry each side until golden brown.

4. Yield 10 cakes.

These Skillet Corn Cakes are solid, filling, and delicious. They must be fried in butter to get the best flavor Add more butter as needed for frying.

You will fill me with *joy* in your presence, with eternal pleasures at your right hand.

Psalm 16:11

DESSERTS

BASIC CREAM PIE

1 (9-inch) deep dish FROZEN PIE SHELL
2 small boxes *COOK AND SERVE* PUDDING
3 c. MILK
1/2 c. SUGAR
1 T. CORNSTARCH
1/2 c. WATER
3 EGG WHITES

1. Bake pie shell according to package directions.

2. Combine milk and pudding mix. Heat, stirring constantly, until a full boil. Pour into pie shell.

3. Combine 2 T. sugar, cornstarch, and water. Cook, stirring constantly, until thick and clear. Place pan in cold water to cool.

4. Beat egg whites to soft peaks. Beat in cornstarch mixture. Gradually add rest of sugar. Beat to stiff peaks. Heap onto filling that has cooled slightly and formed a skin. Spread to seal edges.

5. Bake, uncovered, at 375° for 15 minutes.

CHOCOLATE CREAM PIE

Use chocolate pudding mix.

COCONUT CREAM PIE

Use coconut pudding mix OR vanilla pudding mix with 3/4 c. flaked coconut added after it is cooked. Sprinkle 1/4 c. flaked coconut on top of meringue before baking.

BANANA CREAM PIE

Use vanilla pudding mix. Cool pudding from hot to warm, stirring often to keep skin from forming. Thinly slice two bananas. Cover with lemon/lime soda to keep from turning brown. Drain and add to cooled pudding.

BUTTERSCOTCH PIE

Use butterscotch pudding mix.

LEMON MERINGUE PIE

Use *one* large box lemon cook and serve pudding mix. Prepare according to package directions. I prefer the lemon mix sold by a national company that sells door to door.

Yes, you can make a quick and easy Cream Pie. Brown the crust well so it will not get soggy. This meringue is foolproof! After baking, cool the pie away from drafts. When the pie is room temperature, refrigerate. I do not cover my meringue pies. One large box of pudding mix is *not* equal to two small boxes, so do not substitute.

BREAD PUDDING

4 c. day old BREAD CUBES (4 slices)
1 c. PIE FILLING (from a 21 oz. can)
3 EGGS, beaten slightly
1 (12 oz.) can EVAPORATED MILK
1/3 c. SUGAR

1. Arrange bread cubes in a 7x11-inch pan that has been sprayed with vegetable oil.

2. Cut up fruit in pie filling. Add eggs, milk, and sugar. Beat by hand until well blended.

3. Pour over bread cubes. Press down.

4. Bake, uncovered, at 350° for 30 minutes. Top should be golden brown and knife inserted in center should come out clean. Spread rest of pie filling over top and heat 5 minutes longer. Serve with ice cream or whipped topping.

5. Yield 8 servings.

Because of the egg, keep leftovers refrigerated. We also like to eat this Bread Pudding cold without any toppings. You must try this dessert! It is delicious!

FRENCH APPLE PIE

1 (9-inch) deep dish FROZEN PIE CRUST
1 (21 oz.) can APPLE PIE FILLING
1 c. FLOUR
1/2 c. BROWN SUGAR
1/2 c. (1 stick) BUTTER

1. Cut up apples into bite size pieces with scissors. Spread pie filling into unbaked pie crust.

2. Stir flour and brown sugar together. Cut in butter until crumbs are pea size.

3. Carefully mound crumb mixture on top of pie.

4. Place on foil to catch any drips. Bake at 375° for 1 hour. Cover the topping with foil the last 10 minutes of baking if it is browning too fast.

5. Yield 6 servings.

My family can never wait until this pie cools to eat it. Served plain or with whipped topping or ice cream on top, this will be the best apple pie your family has ever eaten.

FRUIT COBBLER

4 T. (1/2 stick) BUTTER
1 1/2 c. INSTANT BAKING MIX
1 c. SUGAR
1 c. MILK
FRUIT, 1 (16 oz. - 32 oz.) can OR 1 (16 oz.)
    bag frozen, thawed - do *not* drain fruit

1. Put butter in a 9x13-inch pan. Place in oven until butter has melted.

2. Combine baking mix, sugar, and milk. Stir by hand until large lumps are gone. Batter will have many small lumps. Pour over melted butter.

3. Cut up fruit if necessary. Sprinkle fruit and juice over batter. It will sink to the bottom.

4. Bake, uncovered, at 350° for 40 minutes.

You may add 1/3 cup powdered milk to the dry ingredients and then 1 cup water instead of the milk. You can not hurt this cobbler! Frozen fruit will not have much sauce on the bottom. A small can of fruit will have some sauce and a large can will have a lot of sauce. When using sour cherries, sprinkle with 1/4 cup sugar.

GRAHAM CRACKER COOKIES

7 GRAHAM CRACKERS
3/4 c. CHOPPED WALNUTS
3/4 c. BUTTER
3/4 c. BROWN SUGAR
1/2 c. SEMI-SWEET CHOCOLATE
     CHIPS, opt.

1. Break graham crackers into fourths along scored lines. Place in bottom of an ungreased, 9x13-inch pan.

2. Sprinkle nuts over graham crackers.

3. Melt butter. Add brown sugar. Bring to a rapid boil. Boil one minute. Pour over nuts.

4. Bake, uncovered, at 350° for 15 minutes. Remove from oven and sprinkle with chocolate chips if desired. Spread when melted. Remove from pan before completely cooled.

5. Yield 28 cookies.

LEMON SPONGE CAKE

1 (16 oz.) pkg. ANGEL FOOD CAKE MIX
1 (22 oz.) can LEMON PIE FILLING

1. Beat together dry cake mix and pie filling by hand.

2. Pour into a 9x13-inch pan that has been sprayed with vegetable oil.

3. Bake, uncovered, at 350° for 35 minutes. Cake should spring back when touched. Dust with powdered sugar when cool, or serve with ice cream, or whipped topping.

4. Yield 12 servings.

Replace the lemon pie filling with chocolate to make a CHOCOLATE SPONGE CAKE. I sometimes sprinkle 1 c. (6oz.) semi-sweet chocolate chips on top of the chocolate batter before baking. I have also served this cake with chocolate whipped topping. This is easy to make by combining 2 T. chocolate syrup and 1 (8oz.) container of thawed frozen whipped topping.

Fruit pie filling may also be used. The ingredients for this cake are easy to keep on hand for a fast throw together, because they take no refrigeration.

NO MIX BARS

1/2 c. (1 stick) BUTTER
1 c. GRAHAM CRACKER CRUMBS
1 c. (6 oz.) BUTTERSCOTCH CHIPS
1 c. (6 oz.) SEMI-SWEET CHOCOLATE
    CHIPS
1 c. FLAKED COCONUT
1 c. WALNUTS, chopped
1 (14 oz.) can SWEETENED CONDENSED
    MILK

1. Put butter in a 9x13-inch pan. Place in
   oven until butter has melted. Remove
   from oven and sprinkle graham cracker
   crumbs over butter.

2. Sprinkle butterscotch chips, chocolate chips,
   coconut, and nuts on top.

3. Pour sweetened condensed milk over all.

4. Bake, uncovered, at 350° for 30 minutes.

5. Yield 15 bars.

PEANUT BUTTER COOKIES

1 c. SUGAR
1 c. CREAMY PEANUT BUTTER
1 EGG
30 CHOCOLATE KISS CANDIES

1. Combine sugar, peanut butter, and egg.

2. Roll dough into 30 1-inch diameter balls.
   Bake in two batches. Place 15 balls in an
   ungreased, 9x13-inch pan. Unwrap candy kisses
   and gently press one in center of each ball.
   Edges of dough will crack.

3. Bake, uncovered, at 350° for 15 minutes.
   Cool until set before removing from pan.

4. Yield 2 1/2 dozen.

Yes, you have read correctly. There is no flour in these cookies. So simple, your children will be able to make them perfectly without any help. These scrumptious cookies never last long. They are a real treat!

PINEAPPLE UPSIDE DOWN CAKE

1 (20 oz.) can CRUSHED PINEAPPLE, do *not* drain
1 (18 oz.) box YELLOW CAKE MIX
3/4 c. (1 1/2 sticks) BUTTER

1. Spread pineapple with juice over the bottom of a 9x13-inch pan that has been sprayed with vegetable oil.

2. Sprinkle dry cake mix over pineapple with fingers, breaking up any lumps.

3. Cut butter into 1/4-inch pats and arrange on top of cake mix.

4. Bake, uncovered, at 350° for 40 minutes. Cake should be brown on top.

5. Yield 12 servings.

Serve this cake warm or cold, with or without whipped topping. Turn each piece over so the pineapple is on top. It is almost like a bar cookie when cold.

RICE PUDDING

2 1/2 c. WATER
1/2 c. WHITE RICE, uncooked, not instant
1/4 tsp. CINNAMON
1 (14 oz.) can SWEETENED CONDENSED
   MILK

1. Combine water, rice, and cinnamon. Bring to a boil.

2. Add sweetened condensed milk. Boil gently, uncovered, stirring occasionally, until rice absorbs most of the liquid (about 25 minutes). Pudding gets thicker as it cools.

3. Serve hot or cold. Offer milk and cinnamon.

4. Yield 3 cups.

My mother often served hot Rice Pudding covered with milk and sprinkled with cinnamon for dessert when I was a child. It was delicious. I never learned how to make it, because she did not have a recipe. I couldn't seem to dump in the right amounts. This Rice Pudding tastes just like hers did and it comes out the same everytime. After so many years without her Rice Pudding, I ate it every day for two weeks when I first found this recipe.

STRAWBERRY WHIP

1 small box STRAWBERRY GELATIN
1 c. BOILING WATER
1 c. ICE CUBES
1 1/2 c. (4 oz.) FROZEN WHIPPED
    TOPPING, thawed

1. Stir gelatin and boiling water together until gelatin is dissolved.

2. Add ice cubes. Stir until gelatin is slightly thick. Remove any unmelted ice.

3. Add whipped topping. Beat with wire whisk until smooth. Chill.

4. Yield 3 cups.

The whipped topping must be thawed in order to mix in smooth. I like to serve this dessert in individual dishes (clear plastic cups) and garnish with fresh strawberries. It may also be formed in a mold and used as a salad. Any flavor of gelatin may be used for this recipe.

He (God) provides you with plenty of food and fills your hearts with *joy.*

Acts 14:17

INDEX OF RECIPES

BREAKFASTS, CONT.

SOUPS

SANDWICHES

SALADS

VEGETABLES

MAIN DISHES

MAIN DISHES, CONT.

BREADS

DESSERTS

MOM'S TIPS

The ingredients used in these recipes are printed in capital letters to make assembly go fast with just quick glances at the page. You may also take the book to the grocery store to make shopping easier.

You have probably noticed I have not listed any can size fractions except 1/2 oz. 10 3/4 oz. and 11 1/4 oz. are both rounded to 11 oz. I have seen food companies change the sizes of their cans by an ounce or two over the years. For example, a 5 pound bag of sugar is now 4 pounds and a 17 oz. can of corn is now 15 oz.

Oven temperatures vary greatly, especially small camper ovens. Learn to go by how the food looks as to whether it is done or not. Our first camper had an oven that never turned off. I don't know how hot it would have gotten if left to itself! I learned to turn it on and off during baking in order to keep a steady temperature. Buying an oven thermometer will help.

Because space is limited in a camper, I keep my pan sizes simple. The 7x11-inch baking pan fits inside the 9x13-inch baking pan. Inside these I put a set of 4 nested rectangular plastic sealed containers. The sizes are 7 cups, 4 cups, 24 oz. and 12 oz. Clean up is so much easier with non-stick cookware. When buying cookware to keep in the camper, I consider what it would cost to eat out when camping and then I think I am getting a bargain! I keep a set of four pans in the camper. The sizes are 5 qt., 2 qt., 1 qt. and a 12-inch skillet.

The trick to space in a camper is "a place for everything and everything in it's place." This is the only way it will work, so train your family well.

I do not have space in my camper for a muffin tin. I make quick box muffins by baking 2 (7 oz.) boxes or sacks of muffin mix in a 7x11-inch pan. Use 3 for a 9x13-inch pan. To make just 1 box, use the foil muffin cups that stand up by themselves. Place them in a 9x13-inch pan. I also do not have space for a cookie sheet. I have given tips on how to get along without one in the recipes that would normally require one.

I use butter for my cooking and baking because it does not separate. It also gives a better flavor. If you want to use margarine, make sure it has 80% oil or you will be cooking with a lot of flavored water.

Before the camping trip, I often precook the meat I will need. I package it in small plastic bags, label according to recipe, then freeze. This can be done several weeks ahead of time. I have found it so convenient that I sometimes do the same thing for use at home. After a busy day, it is so nice to have a meal that can be easily thrown together.

My husband likes to cook skillet recipes outside on the picnic table. He uses a small gas burner that we have had for years. He is especially good at frying the fish he catches. He coats them with equal parts of flour and corn meal before frying.

Breakfast and camping just go together. We rarely take time to eat breakfast at home, but when we are camping, there is no other way to start the day. Making breakfast is how I wake up my family. They know they may wake up slowly listening to me cook. It was a time for the youngest child to get in bed and cuddle with her dad. Since she is too old, I hope there will soon be grandchildren to take her place.

Children's children are a crown to the aged, and parents are the pride of their children.

Proverbs 17:6

Large plastic totes with lids are perfect to store camping recreational supplies in. The lids keep out dirt and rain so they may be kept outside the camper. Packing the van is easier, because they stack and do not slide off of each other. I keep magazines, novels, nature books, cameras, cassette players, cards, needlepoint, etc... in them year round. I store these containers in a closet in the house when we are not camping. That way I do not have to pack and unpack when we go camping. Men, if you are thinking these sound like heavy containers, my husband will tell you they *are!* But, we don't all fish, now, do we?

A trick to keeping card games after the package has worn out is to put them in a plastic box made for a bar of soap. The cards will last for years stored this way.

We mostly camp in our home state of Kansas, but once a year we travel to Colorado and camp in the mountains. We go to a secluded camp site where there is no water or electricity. We haul water from a nearby town in a 30 gallon tank we keep in the back of the van. The tank is elevated on two by fours. There is a spout underneath of the tank that a hose is attached to. The camper is then filled with water by gravity.

One of my plastic totes is filled with items we use only on our Colorado trip. Forest maps, books about hiking trails, gold mines, hot springs, mountain wild flowers, birds, and tourist attractions are kept together to be brought out once a year and enjoyed. We are always looking for new books to add to our collection.

We have several books on mushrooms. They are fun to look for when we are hiking. We are careful not to touch them with our hands because they can be quite dangerous. We do eat the common morel in Kansas and the bolete in Colorado. There are many others that are edible, but we do not feel we have enough knowledge to eat any but these two that are easily identified.

My first aid supplies are kept the same way as my recreational supplies only I use smaller plastic containers without lids. I have two containers that fit perfectly in a large camper drawer and also fit perfectly on a bathroom cabinet shelf. I keep them stocked with the following: scissors, needle, tweezers, thermometer, sunscreen, insect repellent, antacid, itch cream, laxative pills, diarrhea pills, nausea pills, pain pills, antihistimine, cough drops, eye drops, ear drops, alcohol, antibiotic ointment, petroleum jelly, band aids, styptic stick, Ipecac syrup, dental floss, and a few items that make it unique to our family. If any item is used, it is to be replaced. This is a family rule. That way the boxes are always ready to go.

Make sure to take your health insurance cards with you on your trip. Twice we have had to go to walk in clinics in Colorado. Once, our son had a high temperature for three days straight. His care at the clinic was just as good as if we had been home. Another time, I hurt my back hiking. The doctor at the clinic said I had to spend the next week in bed. The mountains are a lovely place to be bedfast. I had my husband hang a hummingbird feeder outside my bed's window so I could watch them while I took pain medicine and read my favorite books.

I keep two hot water bottles in the camper to warm our feet on those cold nights in the mountains. We also keep warm with hooded sweatshirts. These sweatshirts are for indoor use only so they are always clean to sleep in.

Now, I must say something about cleanliness and camping. It is not an easy thing to maintain especially if water is having to be hauled. Children can use a gallon before we know it just washing their hands! However, because we eat all day long, hands must be kept clean. I keep a box of large baby wipes out on the counter. I take some with us in a plastic bag when we go fishing or on hikes. If we are eating a messy meal like barbecue, the box goes right on the table.

NOTES

NOTES

_____

_____

_____

_____

_____

_____

_____

_____

_____

_____

_____

_____

_____

_____

_____

_____

_____

_____

_____

_____